THIS LAND CALLED AMERICA: **IOWA**

CREATIVE EDUCATION

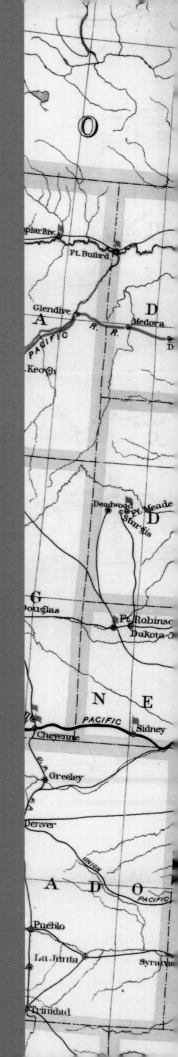

Published by Creative Education
P.O. Box 227, Mankato, Minnesota 56002
Creative Education is an imprint of The Creative Company
www.thecreativecompany.us

Book and cover design by Blue Design (www.bluedes.com)
Art direction by Rita Marshall
Printed in the United States of America

Photographs by Alamy (AGStock USA Inc), Bridgeman Art Library
(Grant Wood), Corbis (Tom Bean, Bettmann, Walter Bibikow/JAI,
David Muench, Maurice Nimmo/Frank Lane Picture Agency, Louie
Psihoyos, Joseph Sohm/Visions of America), Getty Images (Glen
Allison, Kimberly Butler//Time Life Pictures, TIMOTHY A. CLARY/
AFP, John Dominis//Time Life Pictures, Hulton Archive, John Kobal
Foundation, Layne Kennedy, Taylor S. Kennedy/National Geographic,
Steve Liss//Time Life Pictures, William Franklin McMahon//Time Life
Pictures, MPI, Panoramic Images, Spencer Platt)

Library of Congress Cataloging-in-Publication Data
Peterson, Sheryl.
Iowa / by Sheryl Peterson.
p. cm. — (This land called America)
Includes bibliographical references and index.
ISBN 978-1-58341-640-2
1. Iowa—Juvenile literature. I. Title. II. Series.
F621.3.P48 2008
977.7—dc22   2007005686

First Edition
9 8 7 6 5 4 3 2 1

This Land Called America

IOWA

Sheryl Peterson

Iowa

SHERYL PETERSON

EACH FALL IN IOWA, AFTER THE CROPS ARE HARVESTED, FARMERS JUMP ON THEIR TRACTORS. THEY CUT A FEW FIELDS OF CRISP, DRY CORNSTALKS INTO PUZZLES, SOME SHAPED LIKE ANIMALS OR BIRDS. CHILDREN AND ADULTS COME TO HIKE OVER THE CRUNCHY HUSKS. THEY LOVE TROMPING THROUGH TRICKY CORNFIELD MAZES. SUNSHINE WARMS THEIR BACKS AS THEY NAVIGATE THE TWISTY TRAILS, LOOKING FOR THE WAY OUT. MOST OF THE TIME, THEY JUST FIND MORE TALL CORNSTALKS. THE MAZE-GOERS LAUGH AND CHOOSE ANOTHER PATH. FINALLY, THEY CHEER HAPPILY AS THEY SPOT THE EXIT. GETTING LOST IS FUN WHEN IT'S IN AN IOWA CORNFIELD MAZE!

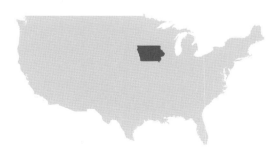

YEAR
1673   French explorers first cross the Mississippi River into Iowa territory.
EVENT

Exploring the Prairie

IN EARLY TIMES, BEFORE IOWA HAD MANY FARMS, THE LAND WAS COVERED WITH FORESTS AND TALL PRAIRIE GRASS. IT WAS THE WILDERNESS HOME OF MANY AMERICAN INDIAN TRIBES. INDIAN PEOPLE OF THE SIOUX AND IOWAY TRIBES HUNTED DEER AND STALKED WILD TURKEYS IN THE FORESTS. THEY GREW BEANS, CORN, AND SQUASH ON THE PRAIRIE.

The prairies of Iowa (opposite) and all land west of the Mississippi became the property of the U.S. with the Louisiana Purchase of 1803.

In 1673, French explorers canoed down the Mississippi River. They were amazed at the rich soil and thick trees they found. More explorers came, and soon the whole Mississippi River territory was claimed by France.

In 1803, France sold the territory to the United States. The deal was called the Louisiana Purchase. President Thomas Jefferson sent scouts to make maps of the new territory. Meriwether Lewis and William Clark canoed into Iowa. The two men found herds of buffalo, rich farmland, and clean water.

In the 1830s, thousands of settlers moved into Iowa. The

YEAR

1682

EVENT

Rene-Robert de La Salle claims the Mississippi River basin, including Iowa, for France.

- 7 -

Large families on the Iowa frontier typically lived for six or seven years in a sod house before building a new one.

A sod house

Indians were not happy to see new people on their land. There was a huge conflict called the Black Hawk War. The Sauk Indians fought against the U.S. Army. Chief Black Hawk was the leader of the Sauk people. In his honor, Iowa is called "The Hawkeye State."

On December 28, 1846, Iowa officially joined the U.S. when President James K. Polk declared Iowa the 29th state in the union. Ansel Briggs became Iowa's first governor. The state's name was taken from the Ioway Indians' language and meant "beautiful land."

More pioneers soon came west for cheap land, wide-open spaces, and adventure. But life on the prairie was hard. Settlers could not find much wood. They dug up the ground to build houses out of sod. Parents and children cleared land and planted potatoes, wheat, and corn. Sometimes there were fires and windstorms. Other times there was not enough water. Diseases such as scarlet fever and smallpox killed many pioneers.

In 1861, the Civil War began. It was a war between the Northern and Southern states over slavery. Even though no battles were fought on Iowa soil, the state sent more than 75,000 men to the Union, or Northern, army. More than 12,000 Iowa soldiers were killed in battle. Many others died of

YEAR

1788 Julien Dubuque, Iowa's first citizen, mines for lead along the Mississippi River in northeastern Iowa.

EVENT

- *9* -

General Grenville Dodge died in Council Bluffs, Iowa, and his home is now a National Historic Landmark.

sickness in the crowded army camps.

One famous soldier from Iowa was General Grenville Dodge. He found spies that wanted to harm the North. Dodge also helped rebuild damaged railroads in the South. Annie Wittenmyer was another important Iowan during this time. She visited her brother in a Union hospital and did not like how the patients were being treated. Wittenmyer worked to get better food for the Civil War soldiers and helped build homes for war orphans.

When the war ended in 1865, Iowans tried to improve their state. They wanted to make everyone's lives easier. Ten years after the Civil War, five railroad lines were built across the state. The railroads linked Iowa with the rest of the country. Trains carried corn, beef, and mail to and from Iowa.

Many Iowans went to Buffalo Bill Cody's Wild West Shows for entertainment. Inside circus tents, Cody and his group acted out Indian battles and horse races. Buffalo Bill was an Iowan who was born near Davenport. When he was a young man, he was a Pony Express Rider. Cody rode his horse all over the territory to deliver mail.

YEAR

1803 The U.S. acquires Iowa in the Louisiana Purchase.

EVENT

Great Plains State

Iowa lies in America's heartland. It is bordered by six states. Minnesota is its northern border. Wisconsin and Illinois are to the east. Missouri lies to the south. Parts of South Dakota and Nebraska form the western boundaries.

Iowa is called a prairie. The
state has deep, rich soil but not
many trees. Iowa's land rises
up to its highest point near
the Iowa-Minnesota border.
The Mississippi River runs
along Iowa's eastern side. The
Big Sioux and Missouri rivers
divide western Iowa from South
Dakota and Nebraska. Iowa's rolling
prairie lies within the Mississippi Valley. It is the
only state bordered on two sides by waterways.

Much of the tall grasses of the pioneer days are gone.
But white-tailed deer and rabbits live in the grassy areas that
remain. Marsh marigolds, prairie lilies, and wild roses (the
state flower) bloom along the roadsides. Forests of birch
and maple trees are found near rivers. Oak trees thrive in the
eastern parts of the state.

The state of Iowa has many mineral resources. Quartzite,
limestone, and gypsum can be found in pastures and along
stream banks or valley sides. Iowa's state rock is the geode.
Geode is a dark stone that has shiny crystals in the middle.

YEAR

| 1833 | Iowa is officially opened for pioneers to build homesteads on the prairie. |

EVENT

I owa has 31 natural lakes. Most of them are in the northwestern part of the state. West Okoboji is the deepest lake. It is a popular summer resort for swimmers and boaters. In the winter, Iowa's frozen lakes attract fishermen. They drill holes in the ice and reel up bluegills, perch, and crappies.

Parts of Iowa have hills that were smoothed out by glaciers. Glaciers were huge ice masses that moved across the land thousands of years ago. Then they melted and left behind large swamps. Settlers drained the swamps to plant crops. Today, 90 percent of Iowa's land is farmland. The state's soil is its most important resource. Iowa leads the nation in corn production. It is also a leader in soybeans, oats, and animal feed.

Ice fishing on a frozen lake (above) may not be popular with more than a select few, but a lonelier place to be is on one of the state's empty back roads (opposite).

Bright flashes of lightning are a common sight during the typically muggy and stormy Iowa summers.

The Mississippi River flows from north to south along Iowa's eastern border for about 300 miles (482.8 km).

Iowans have long, hot summers. The warm weather helps farmers' crops grow. However, summertime can also bring tornadoes. There are no mountains in Iowa to stop gusty winds from howling across the state. Winters in Iowa are cold and often snowy. On average, the state receives about 34 inches (86 cm) of precipitation a year.

Wildlife must be hardy to thrive in Iowa's varying weather. Ring-necked pheasants make their homes in Iowa cornfields. Geese and ducks spend their springs and summers in the state's lakes. Larger animals such as deer can be spotted in Iowa forests.

Iowans believe in protecting their natural resources. Iowa has 83 state parks and 4 state forests. Palisades-Kepler State Park is located near Cedar Rapids in eastern Iowa. Many prehistoric fossils, such as the molar tooth of a mammoth, have been found there. Mammoths were huge creatures that lived on Earth before the glaciers melted.

American Indians lived in Iowa before the first settlers came. One group was called the Mound Builders. These people lived on the prairie overlooking the Mississippi River. They created huge mounds in the ground shaped like birds, bears, or other animals. Visitors to Iowa can view these creations at Effigy Mounds National Monument, located near Harper's Ferry.

YEAR
1846 Iowa becomes the 29th state in the union on December 28.
EVENT

Iowa's Welcome Mat

IN THE 1830S, MANY SETTLERS FELT CROWDED ON THEIR SMALL FARMS IN THE EASTERN U.S. SO LARGE NUMBERS OF IRISH AND GERMAN PIONEERS MADE THE MOVE TO IOWA. NORWEGIAN, SWEDISH, AND DANISH IMMIGRANTS TRAVELED WEST BY TRAIN. THEY ALL CAME TO PLANT CROPS IN THE RICH IOWA SOIL.

The Amish people settled in the southeastern part of the state in the 1840s. This community still thrives in Iowa today. The Amish live a simple life. They drive horse-drawn buggies instead of cars. They wear plain clothing and work the soil with horse-drawn plows. Many Amish sell homemade quilts and handcrafted wooden furniture.

Some people from Germany left their home country so they could worship God as they pleased. They came to Iowa in the 1850s and founded the Amana Colonies. Amana settlers built their homes and shops in east-central Iowa. Like the Amish, they lived simple lives. They owned all their food and

The seven villages of the Amana Colonies are operated like a big business by the Amana Society.

Amish buggies are a common sight along roads in eastern Iowa, especially near Drakesville and Kalona.

Television host Johnny
Carson got his start in
the early 1950s with
a Sunday afternoon
comedy show.

clothing together. Today, the Amana Colonies are a National
Historic Landmark near Iowa City. Tourists visit the Colonies
to watch craftspeople make candles and baskets, build clocks,
and spin woolens.

Iowa is the birthplace of many famous people. The 31st
president of the U.S., Herbert Hoover, was born in West
Branch, Iowa. Mamie Eisenhower, wife of former president
Dwight D. Eisenhower, came from the town of Boone. Iowan
Amelia Jenks Bloomer worked for women's rights in the
1860s and '70s. She wore baggy pants, which people called
"bloomers," under her skirts. Bloomer felt that women should
be able to wear comfortable clothes and work in jobs outside
the home.

Western movie star John Wayne was from Iowa. He was
born in Winterset in 1907. Wayne was called "The Duke,"
and people still enjoy watching his movies. Johnny Carson
was another famous—and funny—Iowan. Carson was on TV
for 30 years as the host of a late-night talk show called *The
Tonight Show*.

Some people think that everyone in Iowa is a farmer.
But that is not true. In fact, Iowa's family farms are slowly
disappearing. They are being replaced by mega-farms that are
owned by big companies. Small farmers often can't compete

YEAR
1856   The first railroad bridge is built across the Mississippi River, connecting Davenport, Iowa, to Rock Island, Illinois.
EVENT

against them. Some Iowans work for the Hy-Vee supermarket chain. Others build John Deere tractors and harvesters. Still others have jobs at the University of Iowa or the Amana Refrigeration Company.

Deere & Company employs thousands of Iowans and is the world's largest maker of farming equipment.

Most Iowans have European backgrounds, but there are other ethnic groups, too. Out of all the American Indian tribes that used to live in Iowa, only one group is left. The Meskwaki, or "people of red earth," live along the Iowa River. They celebrate their culture with traditional pow-wow dancing and storytelling. African Americans were drawn to Iowa in the late 1800s by the coal mines. Today, people from Spanish-speaking countries outnumber African Americans in Iowa.

Bloomers, or loose trousers that were gathered at the ankles, were first worn underneath skirts.

YEAR

| 1890 | Iowa becomes the nation's leading corn producer. |

EVENT

Today, most Iowans live in cities such as Des Moines and Iowa City, but they love the outdoors. People go to the countryside to hike and bike or play golf on one of Iowa's 265 courses. People in Iowa are known for their friendly ways. When Iowa truck drivers pass each other on the highway, they smile and lift a pointer finger off of the wheel. The gesture is called the "Iowa Wave."

From cornfield mazes (above) to showy city landmarks such as Des Moines' state capitol (opposite), Iowans enjoy showing off their state to visitors.

Herbert Hoover is the first person born in Iowa to be elected U.S. president.

Only in Iowa

Iowans are smart Americans; their state has the highest literacy rate in the nation. Eighty-Six percent of Iowans have at least a high-school education. Additionally, the Iowa Braille and Sight-Saving School and the Iowa School for the Deaf provide education for people with vision and hearing impairments.

The University of Iowa in Iowa City is the state's oldest public college. It hosts a famous summer writer's workshop. Writers travel from all over the country to attend. Many well-known authors got their start in Iowa. Novelists such as John Irving and Jane Smiley went on to publish award-winning books after their experience at the workshop.

Iowans love museums and art festivals. Every year, thousands of people visit the MacNider Art Museum in Mason City or walk through the Waterloo Museum of Art. People flock to the James and Meryl Hearst Center in Cedar Falls, too. In 1930, an artist named Grant Wood painted a famous picture called *American Gothic*. He painted it near a little farmhouse in the southeastern town of Eldon, Iowa.

The village where Grant Wood operated a summer art colony is captured in his painting Stone City, Iowa *(1930).*

Living History Farms is in the capital city of Des Moines. It is one of the nation's best outdoor museums. The farm shows how the Ioway Indians lived. It also has models of white settlers' homes. People in Iowa attend many festivals in the

spring and summer. They may go to Nordic Fest in Decorah or Tulip Time in Pella. And in the fall, the Amana Colonies celebrate Octoberfest.

Every summer, Iowans head to Des Moines for the Iowa State Fair. It is the state's largest event. There are thrilling carnival rides and cotton candy. People stroll through livestock shows. They admire prize-winning hogs, sheep, and cattle. At the fair, Iowa farmers learn new ideas from each other and talk about their crops. Other folks catch up on family news and just have fun.

Many Iowans are crazy about sports. Since there are no professional sports teams in the state, people pack the stands for college games. The University of Iowa Hawkeyes have talented football and basketball teams. Their rivals, the Iowa State Cyclones, also thrill fans. Each April, Drake University hosts a track competition. Athletes come to Des Moines from all over the world for the event.

Baseball fans drive to Dyersville, Iowa, the site of the 1989 movie *Field of Dreams*. In the movie, a farmer, played by actor Kevin Costner, cuts a baseball diamond out of his cornfield. Ghosts of famous old-time baseball players come out of the cornstalks to play ball. The film was nominated for an Academy Award for best picture.

YEAR
| 1986 | Justice Linda K. Neuman becomes the first woman to serve on the Iowa Supreme Court. |
EVENT

YEAR
2005
EVENT

Iowa leads the nation in the production of pork, corn, soybeans, and eggs.

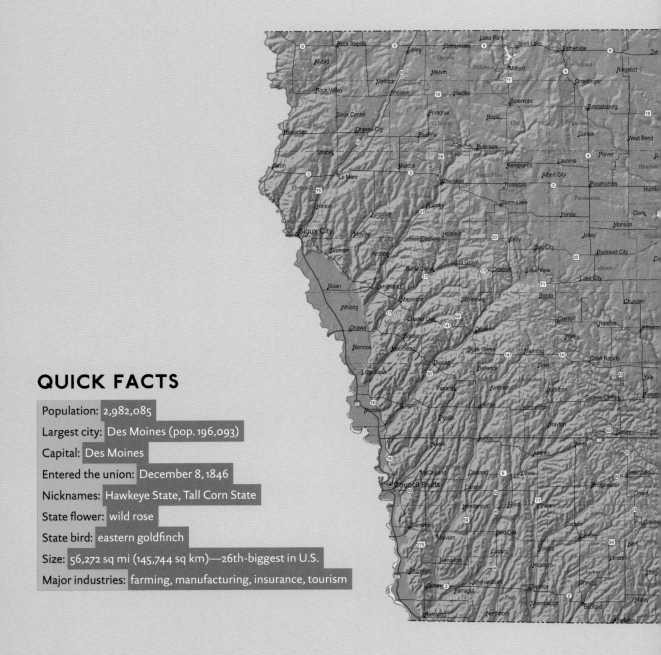

QUICK FACTS

Population: 2,982,085

Largest city: Des Moines (pop. 196,093)

Capital: Des Moines

Entered the union: December 8, 1846

Nicknames: Hawkeye State, Tall Corn State

State flower: wild rose

State bird: eastern goldfinch

Size: 56,272 sq mi (145,744 sq km)—26th-biggest in U.S.

Major industries: farming, manufacturing, insurance, tourism

Iowa has many recreational areas for people to enjoy. Ledges State Park is a popular place in the Des Moines River Valley. It contains American Indian mounds. Wapsipinicon State Park, near Anamosa, is one of the state's oldest parks. Visitors can hike along its sandstone bluffs and explore many caves.

The early natives called Iowa "the beautiful land" for good reason. The state's rolling countryside presents four seasons of nature at its best. Even though it is a modern, growing state, Iowa is still a peaceful place on the prairie. The land between two rivers has historic sites, genuine hospitality, and opportunities for all.

In February, ice storms sweep across northeastern Iowa, leaving about 250,000 people without power.

BIBLIOGRAPHY

Erickson, Lori, and Tracy Stuhr. *Iowa Off the Beaten Path*. Guilford, Conn.: Globe Pequot, 2004.

Hintz, Martin. *Iowa*. Chicago: Children's Press, 2000.

Iowa Tourism Office. "Visiting Iowa." State of Iowa. http://www.iowa.gov/state/main/visiting.html.

Kummer, Patricia. *Iowa*. Mankato, Minn.: Bridgestone Books, 1998.

Marsh, Carole, and Kathy Zimmer. *Iowa: the Iowa Experience*. Atlanta: Gallopade International, 2000.

Smolan, Rick, and David Cohen. *Iowa 24/7*. New York: DK Publishing Inc., 2004.

INDEX